Colophon

©Mathias Jansson (2025)

"Coddled Creativity: Creativity in a World Without Friction"

ISBN 978-91-86915-87-2

Published by:

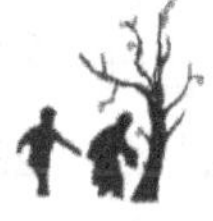
"jag behöver inget förlag"

c/o Mathias Jansson

Tvärvägen 23

232 52 Åkarp

SWEDEN

http://mathiasjansson72.blogspot.se/

Print: Lulu.com

Disclaimer: This book is written with help of ChatGPT. The author has previously conducted extensive research on the subject AI and creativity and contributed with texts in different journals. The texts have been improved, edited and proofread by the author before publishing.

Content

We are entering a new creative era—one where the spark of an idea is often all that's required. The friction that once shaped the creative process—time, skill, failure, repetition—is being smoothed away by generative AI. With a few words typed into a prompt box, we can summon images, compose music, write poetry, and generate entire worlds. The tools that once demanded mastery now offer instant results. Creation has never been so easy.

But what happens when creativity no longer requires craft?

For centuries, human creativity has been inseparable from effort. The painter wrestled with canvas and pigment. The composer labored over melodies and harmonies. The writer revised, rewrote, and reimagined. Creativity was not just about having ideas—it was about shaping them, struggling with them, and sometimes failing to realize them. The process was as important as the product.

Today, that process is being outsourced.

This book explores the rise of what I call coddled creativity—a form of idea generation that is increasingly detached from execution, friction, and failure. It is creativity wrapped in bubble wrap, protected from the discomforts that once defined it. In a world of generative AI, we are encouraged to imagine, but not necessarily to make. We are rewarded for prompts, not persistence.

Through historical reflection, psychological insight, and cultural critique, this book examines how creativity has evolved—and what we risk losing when we no longer need to struggle to create. It asks: What does it mean to be creative in a world where machines do the making? How do we preserve the human spirit of creation when the process becomes optional? And what kind of society are we building when effort is no longer part of the equation?

This is not a book against AI. It is a book for creativity.

Before creativity became a buzzword, it was a necessity. Long before we spoke of innovation, ideation, or disruption, humans created because they had to—tools to hunt, shelters to survive, stories to remember. Creativity was not a luxury or a personality trait. It was a way of being in the world.

In ancient societies, the act of making was deeply physical. The potter shaped clay with bare hands. The weaver worked thread by thread. The builder lifted stone. These acts were slow, deliberate, and often painful. But they were also deeply human. The process of creation was inseparable from the body, from time, and from the limitations of the material world.

Even as civilizations advanced, creativity remained connected to effort. The Renaissance painter spent years mastering perspective. The composer labored over symphonies with ink and paper. The writer revised manuscripts by candlelight. Creativity was not just about having ideas—it was about realizing them through skill, patience, and persistence.

Take Ludwig van Beethoven, for example. His *Symphony No. 9*, one of the most celebrated works in Western music, took over a decade to conceptualize and complete. He worked through increasing deafness, isolation, and depression. The final choral movement—*Ode to Joy*—was not just a musical triumph, but a testament to human resilience.

Beethoven didn't just have an idea; he fought to bring it to life.

Or consider Leonardo da Vinci, whose notebooks reveal a mind constantly wrestling with form, function, and failure. His painting *The Last Supper* was plagued by technical problems, including the experimental technique he used that began to deteriorate almost immediately. He spent years studying anatomy, light, and geometry—not to generate ideas, but to earn the right to execute them.

Even in modern times, the struggle remains central. Vincent van Gogh created over 2,000 artworks in just over a decade, many of which were made in poverty and mental anguish. His brushstrokes were not the result of a single inspired moment, but of relentless experimentation and emotional intensity. He sold only one painting in his lifetime.

Creativity, at its core, is not just about producing something new—it's about transformation. And transformation rarely happens without resistance.

Throughout history, the most profound creative breakthroughs have emerged not from ease, but from tension. The sculptor chips away at stone, not knowing if the form will emerge. The writer stares at the blank page, wrestling with doubt. The composer hears fragments of melody in their mind, unsure how to weave them into harmony. These moments of uncertainty, frustration, and failure are not obstacles to creativity—they are its crucible.

Mistakes, in this context, are not failures. They are feedback. They are the unexpected turns that force the creator to see differently, think differently, and ultimately become different. When a painter misplaces a stroke, it may lead to a new texture. When a dancer stumbles, it may reveal a new rhythm. When a writer deletes a paragraph, it may open space for a deeper truth.

This is the paradox of creative struggle: it hurts, but it heals. It frustrates, but it teaches. It slows us down, but it deepens us.

Consider Igor Stravinsky, whose *The Rite of Spring* caused riots at its premiere in 1913. The music was so radically different—so rhythmically violent and harmonically dissonant—that audiences couldn't accept it. But Stravinsky didn't retreat. He leaned into the discomfort, and in doing so, reshaped the future of music.

Or Frida Kahlo, whose paintings were born from physical pain and emotional trauma. Her art was not an escape from suffering—it was a confrontation with it. Her broken body became a canvas for resilience, identity, and defiance.

These artists didn't just create—they endured. And through that endurance, they discovered new ways of seeing, feeling, and expressing.

In a world increasingly optimized for ease, we risk losing this depth. When AI removes the friction, it also removes the opportunity for growth. If we no longer struggle to make, we may no longer evolve through making. Creativity becomes a transaction, not a transformation.

But the soul of creativity lies in the process, not just the product. It is in the long nights, the failed drafts, the broken brushes, the missed notes. It is in the moment when the creator almost gives up—but doesn't. That is where the real art lives.

Every age believes it has discovered freedom. But freedom, in art, is rarely given. It is earned through struggle — through the act of pushing against what already exists. The history of creativity is not a story of continuous progress, but of confrontation: with materials, with rules, with the past, and sometimes with the self.

Art does not evolve because it becomes easier. It evolves because someone decides that ease is no longer enough.

In the classical world, art was a matter of mastery. Painters learned geometry and proportion. Composers followed strict counterpoint. Writers adhered to form and meter. Beauty was defined by balance and control. Creativity meant working within a framework, not breaking it.

Yet even within this structure, there was tension. The artist always wrestled with the limitations of convention — with the gap between what could be expressed and what had not yet been imagined.

Michelangelo described sculpting as a process of release: he did not create the figure, he freed it from the stone. But that release came through friction — through the resistance of marble, through years of discipline. His genius was not effortless inspiration, but the transformation of resistance into revelation.

Every generation inherits this tension. Each must decide whether to preserve what has been achieved or to destroy it in search of something new.

At the turn of the twentieth century, a young painter from Málaga began to question what painting was supposed to be. Pablo Picasso had already mastered academic realism by the age of sixteen. But mastery no longer satisfied him. He began to unlearn, to break form, to distort. In *Les Demoiselles d'Avignon* (1907), he shattered perspective and fractured the human body into planes and edges. The work was considered grotesque, even offensive.

Yet it became the starting point for modern art.

Picasso's innovation did not come from abandoning tradition, but from confronting it. He broke painting only because he had learned to build it. His rebellion was not rejection — it was transformation through resistance. The same could be said of Claude Monet's *Impression, Sunrise* (1872), whose loose brushstrokes and unfinished surfaces scandalized critics. They saw laziness; he saw light.

In both cases, the act of struggle — against expectation, against mastery — became the source of renewal.

The same pattern unfolds in music. When Ludwig van Beethoven premiered his later works, audiences were bewildered. The *Grosse Fuge*, written when he was almost completely deaf, was called incomprehensible. Even his publisher asked him to write something "more pleasing." But Beethoven refused. The music was not meant to please; it was meant to break open.

And when John Cage presented *4'33"* (1952) — four minutes and thirty-three seconds of silence — he forced audiences to confront their own expectations of sound. Cage was not offering emptiness. He was redefining what music could mean.

Every revolution in art begins this way: with an act of disobedience.

Literature follows the same rhythm of rupture. James Joyce's *Ulysses* dismantled the structure of the novel, replacing plot with consciousness. Virginia Woolf's *To the Lighthouse* turned narrative into interior monologue. Samuel Beckett reduced theatre to almost nothing — a voice, a gesture, a silence.

Each writer faced resistance not only from the public but from language itself. They fought to make words express what words could not yet contain. Their breakthroughs were not the result of effortless inspiration, but of confrontation with the limits of form.

To struggle with expression is to renew it.

This cycle of mastery and rebellion — of learning, breaking, and rebuilding — defines human creativity. Art thrives on tension because tension keeps it alive.

Without struggle, there is no evolution. Without resistance, there is no reason to move.

Innovation, in this sense, is an emotional process as much as a technical one. It requires discomfort — the feeling that what exists is no longer enough. Artists have always used that discomfort as fuel, transforming dissatisfaction into discovery.

The creative act is therefore not only an act of production, but of opposition. It is the refusal to accept what is given. It is the decision to search for meaning when meaning has become too familiar.

In the age of AI, this pattern is under threat. Generative systems do not struggle. They do not face resistance. They do not tire, fail, or despair. They produce novelty without need, invention without intention. They can generate endless variations, but they cannot revolt against themselves.

True artistic renewal — the kind that reshapes culture — requires more than variation. It requires the ability to feel constraint and to reject it. It requires frustration, dissatisfaction, and the courage to change direction. These are human capacities, born from the experience of limitation.

AI can replicate styles, but not the tension that made those styles necessary. It can generate a Cubist painting, but not the need that drove Picasso to fracture the human form. It can imitate silence, but not Cage's intent to make us listen.

The machine can produce what once broke the rules, but it cannot decide to break them again.

Every generation must rediscover the meaning of creativity. For centuries, that meaning has been tied to struggle — to the willingness to face difficulty, to question convention, to risk failure. Without that struggle, art risks becoming repetition.

Breaking the frame is not an act of destruction for its own sake. It is an act of renewal — the way creativity reminds itself that it is alive.

And in a world increasingly optimized for comfort and automation, the next revolution in art may not come from the machine that creates, but from the human who dares to resist it.

In the modern creative landscape, ideas have become the currency of innovation. We celebrate the brainstorm, the pitch, the concept. We gather in rooms filled with sticky notes and whiteboards, encouraged to "think big," "disrupt," and "dream without limits." The idea has become the hero of the story.

But somewhere along the way, the act of making began to fade.

This shift—from process to concept, from craft to idea—marks a profound change in how we understand creativity. In the past, ideas were seeds. They required soil, water, time, and care. Today, they are often treated as finished products. The assumption is that once the idea exists, the rest will follow—either by delegation, automation, or AI.

This is the essence of idea culture: a system that rewards imagination but often neglects execution.

In corporate environments, this manifests as innovation departments that generate endless proposals but rarely build prototypes. In education, students are praised for creative thinking but not always taught the discipline of iteration. In social media, creators are celebrated for concepts that go viral, regardless of depth or durability.

Generative AI has amplified this trend.

With tools like ChatGPT, Midjourney, and Suno, the gap between idea and output has collapsed. A single sentence can generate a song, a painting, a business plan. The friction is gone. The process is instant. And while this opens extraordinary possibilities, it also reinforces the notion that the idea is enough.

But creativity without execution is incomplete.

Ideas are not inherently valuable. They gain meaning through context, refinement, and realization. A novel concept may be exciting, but until it is shaped, tested, and brought into the world, it remains potential—not impact.

Moreover, the overemphasis on ideas can lead to creative fragility. When creators are shielded from the realities of making—deadlines, constraints, criticism—they may struggle to develop resilience. They may become addicted to novelty, chasing the next idea without ever finishing the last. They may fear failure, because they've never had to face it.

This is where *coddled creativity* begins to take root.

In a world that celebrates ideation but avoids execution, we risk raising a generation of creators who are brilliant in theory but untested in practice. We risk losing the wisdom that comes from doing, failing, and trying again. We risk mistaking imagination for mastery.

To reclaim creativity as a meaningful force, we must restore balance. We must honor the idea—but also the labor. We must teach that creativity is not just about what you think, but what you build. And we must remember that the most powerful ideas are not the ones that come easily, but the ones that survive the process.

In 1917, Marcel Duchamp submitted a porcelain urinal to an art exhibition under the pseudonym R. Mutt. He titled it *Fountain*. It was not sculpted, painted, or altered in any significant way. It was a readymade object—mass-produced, functional, and utterly ordinary. Yet Duchamp's gesture would become one of the most radical turning points in the history of art.

With *Fountain*, Duchamp posed a provocative question: What makes something art? Is it the object itself, or the idea behind it? Is it the hand of the artist, or the context in which the object is placed? By removing the need for craftsmanship, Duchamp elevated the concept above the material. The artist became a thinker, a provocateur, a curator of meaning.

This moment marked the beginning of a profound shift: the rise of conceptual art.

In the decades that followed, artists increasingly challenged the notion that art had to be handmade, beautiful, or even permanent. Sol LeWitt famously declared, "The idea becomes a machine that makes the art." His wall drawings were often executed by others, following written instructions. The artist's role was to conceive, not to construct.

Joseph Kosuth's *One and Three Chairs* (1965) presented a physical chair, a photograph of the chair, and a dictionary definition of "chair." The work was not about the object—it was about the language, the representation, and the idea of the object. Art became a philosophical inquiry.

By the late 20th century, this shift had expanded into relational aesthetics, a term coined by curator Nicolas Bourriaud. Artists like Rirkrit Tiravanija created works that were not objects at all, but experiences—like cooking and serving Thai curry in a gallery space. The artwork was the interaction, the social exchange, the moment shared. The audience became co-creators.

In this new paradigm, the handicraft of art was no longer central. What mattered was the framework, the intention, the disruption of norms. The artist was not a maker, but a facilitator of meaning.

This evolution mirrored broader cultural changes. As society became more conceptual, more digital, more abstract, so did art. The rise of theory, media, and networks shifted focus from the tangible to the symbolic. Art became less about what it is, and more about what it means.

But this shift also raised questions.

What happens when the idea is everything, and the making is nothing? Can art survive without touch, time, or technique? Does the absence of struggle diminish the depth of expression?

In many ways, the art world anticipated the very conditions we now face with generative AI. Today, anyone can generate an image, a poem, or a melody with a few clicks. The conceptual has triumphed. The process has been outsourced. The artist, once a laborer of form, is now a prompt engineer.

For centuries, we have believed that great art is born out of suffering. The painter's despair, the poet's melancholy, the composer's torment — all have been woven into the mythology of creativity. The artist has not only been admired for what they made, but for what they endured. Pain became proof of authenticity. Struggle became a kind of currency.

From Van Gogh's self-portraits to Sylvia Plath's confessional poetry, from Beethoven's deafness to Basquiat's collapse, we have learned to see biography as the key to understanding art. The story behind the work gives it depth. The life of the artist gives it meaning. We do not only look at the painting — we look through it, searching for the human who made it.

This mythology of genius has shaped how we value art. The artist is seen as a conduit for something beyond the ordinary, touched by inspiration but marked by fragility. The "genius" stands apart: gifted, restless, often misunderstood. Their suffering is not incidental — it is integral to the myth. Creativity, in this view, is not just production. It is sacrifice.

But what happens when creation no longer requires suffering?

Generative AI produces art without biography. It creates beauty without a life behind it. There is no memory, no pain, no history in the algorithm. It can imitate style, structure, and form, but not the experience that once gave those forms weight. The painting has no painter. The poem has no author.

In this new condition, the myth of genius begins to unravel. We can still admire the result, but we cannot locate its origin. We can be moved by the image, but not by the story of its making — because there is none. The artwork no longer testifies to struggle, discipline, or emotion. It simply exists, generated by code that knows no despair, no doubt, no joy.

An AI can reproduce Van Gogh's brushstrokes, but not his longing. It can echo Plath's syntax, but not her consciousness. It can model genius, but not live it. The connection between life and art — between the inner world of the creator and the outer expression of the work — is lost. What remains is surface: a simulation of feeling without a source.

When creativity becomes detached from the human story, it risks losing its moral dimension. The myth of genius has always been a story of becoming — of transformation through hardship. It has taught us that beauty requires something of us: time, effort, and sometimes suffering. AI short-circuits that process. It produces the result without the journey.

The myth of effortless genius is not new. It has existed in different forms throughout history — in tales of divine inspiration, in the Romantic cult of the artist, in the modern fascination with talent. But in every version, the myth still depended on humanity. The genius struggled because they were human. Their imperfection gave their work depth.

AI reverses that equation. It offers perfection without effort, mastery without failure, fluency without struggle. But what is left when the artist no longer struggles? If creativity no longer costs anything, does it still mean anything?

Art, at its core, has never been about ease. It has been about resistance — the resistance of materials, of form, of self. The artist shapes the work, but the work also shapes the artist. The friction between the two is what gives art its vitality. Without that friction, creation becomes reproduction.

As AI becomes more deeply integrated into culture, the idea of genius may evolve. Perhaps the new genius will not be the maker, but the mediator — the one who gives context and meaning to machine-made forms. The role of the artist may shift from producing to interpreting, from creating to framing. But the myth of the suffering genius — of art as transformation through difficulty — will remain a powerful undercurrent. It speaks to something fundamental in us: the belief that struggle deepens experience, and that art without struggle cannot truly be alive.

Generative AI will continue to challenge that belief. It will produce more, faster, with greater precision and variety. But the hunger for the human story will persist. We will still look for traces of intention, emotion, and vulnerability in what we see. We will still want to know that someone, somewhere, cared enough to make it — and risked something in the process.

Because art, in the end, is not only about what is made. It is about who we become in the act of making.

We are now living in a world where the act of creation has been reduced to a sentence.

A few words typed into a prompt box can generate a painting, a symphony, a short story, a business plan, a logo, a voice. The tools are no longer passive—they are generative. They do not wait for our hands to shape them; they respond to our thoughts, our whims, our fragments of intention. The creative process has become conversational, instantaneous, and—perhaps most radically—detached from skill.

This is the age of prompted creativity.

In previous chapters, we explored how technology gradually thinned the barrier between idea and execution. But generative AI has collapsed it entirely. The friction is gone. The process is outsourced. The maker is now a selector, a curator, a refiner of outputs. The creative act begins and ends with a prompt.

This shift is not just technical—it is psychological.

When we no longer need to struggle to create, we begin to think differently about what creativity is. We may start to believe that the idea alone is enough. That the first draft is the final product. That the machine knows better. We may lose the patience to iterate, the resilience to fail, the curiosity to explore.

We may lose the creative self.

Generative AI invites us to imagine without making, to express without effort, to produce without process. And while this opens extraordinary possibilities—especially for those previously excluded from creative industries—it also risks flattening the depth of human expression. When everything is possible instantly, nothing feels necessary.

The danger is not that AI will replace artists. The danger is that it will replace the conditions that make artistry meaningful.

Creativity has always been a dialogue between the inner and outer world—between impulse and resistance, inspiration and limitation. It is in the tension between what we want to say and what we struggle to express that art is born. When that tension disappears, so does the transformation.

In a world increasingly designed to eliminate discomfort, failure has become something to avoid. Mistakes are corrected instantly. AI anticipates our needs, smooths our errors, and guides us toward optimal outcomes. The creative process, once defined by trial and error, is now curated for efficiency.

But psychology tells a different story.

Failure is not a flaw in the system—it is the system. It is the mechanism through which we learn, grow, and evolve. And in the realm of creativity, it is essential.

Jean Piaget's theory of cognitive development emphasizes the importance of *disequilibrium*—the moment when a person's understanding of the world is challenged. This discomfort forces the mind to reorganize, adapt, and construct new knowledge. In creative work, disequilibrium is not a disruption—it is a catalyst. When a painting fails to evoke emotion, when a melody feels unresolved, when a story collapses under its own weight, the creator is pushed to rethink, revise, and reimagine.

Lev Vygotsky's concept of the *Zone of Proximal Development* (ZPD) adds another layer. Learning happens most powerfully in the space between what we can do alone and what we can do with support. But this zone requires challenge. It requires effort. It requires the possibility of failure. In a world where AI removes the need for help—by simply doing the task for us—the ZPD collapses. We no longer stretch ourselves. We no longer need guidance. We no longer learn.

Carol Dweck's research on *growth mindset* shows that people who believe their abilities can be developed through effort and learning are more likely to persevere, take risks, and achieve long-term success. Those with a *fixed mindset*, who believe talent is innate and failure is shameful, often avoid challenge and stagnate. Generative AI, when used without reflection, can reinforce a fixed mindset. If the machine always knows best, why try? If the first result is good enough, why revise? If failure is never allowed, why risk anything at all?

Mihaly Csikszentmihalyi's theory of *flow*—the state of deep immersion in a task—depends on a balance between challenge and skill. If the challenge disappears, so does the flow. If the process becomes too easy, it becomes meaningless. AI may offer instant results, but it cannot replicate the psychological depth of flow, which emerges from sustained effort and engagement.

In a world increasingly optimized for ease and perfection, we risk losing the very friction that fuels human development. Failure and resistance are not obstacles to be eliminated—they are the raw materials of growth. They challenge our assumptions, stretch our capacities, and deepen our engagement with the world. From Piaget's disequilibrium to Vygotsky's ZPD, from Dweck's growth mindset to Csikszentmihalyi's flow, the message is clear: discomfort is not a defect—it is a design feature of learning and creativity. To truly evolve, we must embrace the imperfect, the difficult, and the uncertain. Because it is in the struggle—not the shortcut—that we become more fully human.

Generative AI has opened the floodgates of creativity. With a few words, anyone can summon images, music, stories, and designs. The tools are powerful, accessible, and increasingly intuitive. But beneath this surface of abundance lies a quieter shift—one that may reshape the very nature of artistic expression.

As AI becomes a central part of the creative process, it also becomes a filter. And filters, by design, exclude.

Generative AI systems are trained on existing data— millions of artworks, songs, texts, and styles. These systems learn what is statistically likely, what is popular, what is coherent. When prompted, they generate outputs that reflect these patterns. The result is often impressive, but rarely surprising.

This creates a feedback loop:

- Users prompt the AI.
- The AI generates something familiar.
- Users select what they like.
- The system reinforces those patterns.

Over time, this loop narrows the creative space. Novelty becomes less likely. The system learns to optimize for what works, not for what challenges. As a result, creativity becomes safer, smoother, and more predictable.

A 2025 meta-analysis of 28 studies involving over 8,000 participants found that while humans collaborating with generative AI performed better on creative tasks than those working alone, the diversity of ideas significantly declined in such collaborations. This suggests that while AI can enhance productivity and ideation, it may also narrow the creative space, pushing users toward more predictable outputs.

Another large-scale study of over 50,000 users using text-to-image AI tools revealed that while creative productivity increased by 50%, average novelty in both content and visual style declined over time. Artists who successfully explored new ideas and filtered AI outputs for coherence were evaluated more favorably by their peers, but overall, the system encouraged stylistic convergence.

These findings reinforce a central concern: when creativity becomes frictionless, it risks becoming formulaic.

Psychologists define *divergent thinking* as the ability to generate multiple, varied, and original ideas. It is a core component of creativity. But AI systems are not designed to think divergently—they are designed to predict. They generate what is most probable, not what is most unexpected.

Unless users actively push the system toward novelty—by experimenting, remixing, or rejecting default outputs—the AI will tend to produce convergent results.

Just as social media creates information bubbles, generative AI creates aesthetic bubbles. If the system learns your preferences, it will tailor outputs to match them. This personalization can be comforting—but it also risks limiting exposure to unfamiliar styles, ideas, and perspectives.

In such a system:

- You see what you like.
- You are served more of it.
- You stop encountering what challenges you.

Art becomes a mirror, not a window.

This undermines one of the most important functions of creativity: to disrupt, to provoke, to expand perception. Without friction, without surprise, creativity becomes a form of confirmation.

Generative AI excels at scale. It can produce thousands of variations in seconds. But this scale comes at a cost. The uniqueness of a work—the personal struggle, the emotional depth, the intentional imperfection—is often lost in the process.

Art becomes content. Creativity becomes output. And the artist becomes a curator of prompts, rather than a maker of meaning.

This shift echoes the concerns raised in previous chapters: when creativity becomes frictionless, it risks becoming formulaic. When the process is optimized, the soul of the work may be flattened.

To preserve the richness of human creativity, we must resist the temptation to only create what is already liked. We must:

- Use AI critically, not just conveniently.
- Embrace error, friction, and surprise.
- Seek out the unfamiliar.
- Value process over product.

Creativity is not just about making—it is about becoming. And becoming requires struggle.

The first generation of artists to embrace generative AI did not grow up with it. They came from a world of friction—where creativity was earned through repetition, failure, and slow mastery. They remember what it meant to struggle with form, to wrestle with tools, to make mistakes that taught them something deeper than technique: patience, humility, and resilience.

These artists learned the hard way.

They spent years refining their craft. They failed publicly. They revised endlessly. They knew the weight of a blank canvas, the silence of writer's block, the frustration of a broken loop in a composition. And when generative AI arrived, they didn't see it as a replacement—they saw it as a shortcut. A tool to accelerate ideation, to explore variations, to push boundaries. But they still knew how to build from scratch.

For them, AI is a collaborator, not a crutch.

They use it to prototype, to experiment, to break through creative walls. But they also know when to step away from the machine. They understand that the most meaningful work often comes from the parts AI can't reach: intuition, emotion, contradiction. Their creativity is layered—rooted in experience, enriched by technology.

Then came the next generation.

These are the artists who grew up with AI. For them, the prompt box is not a novelty—it's the starting point. They've never had to struggle with perspective drawing, music theory, or narrative structure. AI can fix their mistakes before they even make them. It can guide them toward the "right" answer, the "best" composition, the "most engaging" style.

They are served by the machine.

This generation is fluent in tools, but often untested in process. They may never experience the slow burn of mastery, the sting of failure, or the joy of solving a problem through effort alone. Their creativity is fast, fluid, and frictionless. But what does that mean for the future of art?

Will it be more conformist, shaped by algorithms trained on what's popular, what's liked, what's optimized? Or will it be more diverse, empowered by access, experimentation, and the ability to remix the entire history of art in seconds?

The answer is not simple. AI can democratize creativity, but it can also homogenize it. It can open doors, but it can also guide everyone through the same hallway. When mistakes are eliminated, learning may become shallow. When effort is optional, growth may be stunted. When the machine knows best, the artist may stop asking questions.

Imagine a future where you no longer need to create—because creation happens for you.

You wake up, and your personal AI has already generated a gallery of images tailored to your taste. Music composed in your favorite style plays softly in the background. A story unfolds on your screen, written in the tone and genre you most enjoy. You didn't ask for any of it. You simply exist, and the machine knows what you want.

This is not science fiction. It is the logical extension of where we're headed.

In this future, creativity becomes responsive. You don't need to imagine what you want to see, hear, or feel. You only need to wish—and often, not even that. AI systems, trained on your preferences, behaviors, and emotional patterns, anticipate your desires. They generate endless variations of art, music, literature, and experience—each one more attuned to your taste than the last.

You are no longer the creator. You are the receiver.

At first, this seems utopian. Everyone has access to beauty, meaning, and expression. No one is excluded by lack of skill, time, or resources. The machine becomes a mirror, reflecting your inner world back to you in infinite forms.

But there is a danger in this mirror.

When we only see what we want, we stop seeing what we need. When art is tailored to our preferences, we may never encounter the unfamiliar, the uncomfortable, the challenging. We may never be provoked, disrupted, or transformed. We may never step outside our safe zone.

Art has always been a way to stretch the soul—to confront new ideas, to feel what others feel, to see through different eyes. It is not just a comfort—it is a confrontation. It asks us to grow. But in a world of wishful creation, growth may become optional.

This future risks becoming a feedback loop of taste. AI learns what you like, gives you more of it, refines it, perfects it, and repeats. The result is not diversity—it is personalized conformity. Each person lives in a curated aesthetic bubble, surrounded by art that agrees with them.

What happens to learning in such a world?

Mistakes, once essential to growth, are eliminated. AI corrects your grammar, balances your composition, harmonizes your melody. You never have to fail. You never have to try again. You never have to wonder if you're doing it right—because the machine already knows.

This may lead to a generation of creators who are technically fluent but creatively fragile. They may produce more, but risk understanding less. They may express more, but feel less. They may innovate less—

not because they lack imagination, but because they've never had to fight for it.

The future of art in this world is uncertain.

Will it become more diverse, as billions of individuals generate unique expressions of their inner lives? Or will it become more uniform, shaped by algorithms that optimize for engagement, comfort, and familiarity?

Throughout history, some of the most revered works of art began their lives as provocations, shocking audiences and angering critics. Michelangelo's *David* scandalized Florentine society with its naked audacity; Édouard Manet's *Le Déjeuner sur l'herbe* scandalized Parisian salons with its casual eroticism and audacious realism; Stravinsky's *The Rite of Spring* provoked riots at its premiere in 1913. In literature, James Joyce's *Ulysses* was banned for obscenity, while Gustave Flaubert's *Madame Bovary* faced trial for its candid portrayal of adultery.

These works share a common thread: they pushed boundaries, challenged norms, and confronted their audiences with uncomfortable truths. The offense they caused was not incidental—it was central to their impact. Art's capacity to provoke, to unsettle, is a key part of its power. And yet, over time, these once-controversial works have often become canonical, celebrated, and even beloved. What was once scandal is now esteemed. Society's shock at the audacity of these creations has faded, leaving only admiration for their vision and craftsmanship.

Today, however, we live in a very different cultural moment. The rise of social media, global connectivity, and heightened awareness of social injustices has created a cultural climate in which offense is often avoided at all costs. Institutions, brands, and creators increasingly preemptively sanitize their work to ensure that no one feels attacked, uncomfortable, or alienated. Comedy is softened, visual art is moderated, literature is carefully edited. The goal is noble on the surface: to create a society where no one feels harmed by expression. But the unintended consequence may be a profound narrowing of the artistic landscape.

When all art is made "safe," it risks losing the very quality that makes it transformative. Provocation, discomfort, and challenge are not flaws—they are mechanisms through which art can expand our perspectives, ignite debate, and reveal truths about ourselves and the world. Art that never offends may entertain, comfort, or please, but it seldom changes minds or shakes society. The classics of the past remind us that pushing boundaries is not an optional luxury for art—it is often essential.

By shielding audiences from offense, we risk erasing the very friction that drives cultural growth. We risk cultivating a society in which creativity is coddled, never tested, and ultimately muted. The provocative work of the past serves as a reminder that enduring art often emerges from tension, struggle, and the courage to challenge prevailing norms. To honor that legacy, contemporary creators must resist the impulse to sanitize and instead embrace the risk of provocation, trusting that future generations will recognize the value of daring expression—even if it is uncomfortable in the moment.

Art has always been a mirror held up to society. Sometimes that mirror reflects a truth that stings. But the sting is not failure—it is proof that art is alive, relevant, and capable of moving hearts and minds.

Every technological revolution begins with wonder. The first photographs were seen as miracles. The first films, as magic. The first social networks promised connection without distance. And now, generative AI promises creativity without effort. Each time, the promise feels irresistible — at least for a while.

But wonder fades. What once felt like liberation begins to feel like confinement. We realize that tools designed to free us can also start to define us.

The story of social media offers a useful warning. In its early years, it was a place of discovery and play — a digital commons where anyone could share, connect, and express. Over time, the platforms grew, commercialized, and optimized. The algorithms learned what we liked, what kept us scrolling, what made us react. Gradually, the open space of expression became a system of prediction and control.

What had started as a tool for connection turned into an engine of comparison. What had promised authenticity began to reward performance. What had offered community became a marketplace for attention.

Today, many young people are leaving these platforms. They are tired of being watched, measured, and sold. They describe feeling anxious, lonely, and creatively drained. The feed that once inspired them now makes them feel smaller. The performance of self has replaced the experience of being.

Something similar may happen with generative AI.

At first, the novelty of effortless creation will be intoxicating. We will generate endless songs, images, and stories — each one smooth, coherent, and instantly shareable. But over time, the very ease that attracts us will begin to feel hollow. When everything is possible, nothing feels essential. When every image can be made in seconds, the image loses its weight.

Just as social media has begun to exhaust its users, AI may begin to exhaust its creators. The pleasure of instant output will fade when we realize that creation without friction produces expression without depth. We may begin to miss the slow struggle of making — the imperfect gesture, the failed attempt, the small victory earned through persistence.

Humans have always sought meaning through effort. We climb mountains not because it is efficient, but because it is difficult. We write by hand, even when we could dictate, because the slowness helps us think. We create not only to show what we can do, but to discover who we are. When technology removes all resistance, it removes part of that discovery.

The return to making will not be a rejection of technology, but a rebalancing. Just as some people now turn away from social media toward smaller, slower spaces — handwritten letters, local communities, physical crafts — we may see a similar shift in art. Artists may seek materials that resist automation: clay, ink, performance, noise. They may value process over product, limitation over abundance, time over speed.

Already, a quiet counterculture is forming. Musicians are recording on analog equipment. Photographers are returning to film. Writers are printing small zines instead of posting online. These gestures are not nostalgic; they are acts of reclamation. They assert that creativity is not just about what we make, but how we make it — and how the making changes us.

The next creative movement may not be defined by technology, but by refusal. Refusal to optimize, to automate, to outsource the parts of art that hurt and teach. In a world that generates images by the millions, the most radical act may be to draw one by hand.

We will take back creativity not because we have to, but because we need to. We need friction to feel alive. We need difficulty to measure growth. We need the slow rhythm of making to remind us of our place in time.

When the novelty of AI fades — as it surely will — we will look again for what cannot be generated: the tremor in the line, the imperfection in the voice, the trace of a human hand.

Because what makes art human is not the idea or the outcome. It is the distance between what we imagine and what we can achieve — the space where we try, fail, and try again.

That space is where meaning lives. And one way or another, we will find our way back to it.

We are living in an age of coddled creativity. We are surrounded by tools that protect us from failure, friction, and uncertainty. With a few words, we can generate an image, a poem, or a melody. The process that once required time, patience, and persistence now unfolds effortlessly. We are encouraged to imagine, but not to struggle; to produce, but not to wrestle with the act of making.

At first, this comfort feels like progress. The machines promise liberation — freedom from drudgery, from imperfection, from doubt. But creativity without resistance is not liberation. It is sedation. When every difficulty is removed, we also remove the depth that comes from overcoming it.

Coddled creativity risks turning art into simulation — beautiful, coherent, and empty. It offers the form of imagination without the friction that gives imagination meaning. The mistake is not in using these tools, but in believing that ease can replace engagement, that fluency can replace feeling.

Friction has always been the teacher of creativity. When the brush hesitates, when the sentence collapses, when the melody refuses to resolve — that is where understanding begins. To make art is to confront resistance and be changed by it. It is not the avoidance of difficulty that makes us creative, but our willingness to meet it.

AI can assist us, but it cannot endure for us. It cannot experience the tension between failure and discovery that defines human making. It can generate what looks like art, but it cannot carry the weight of effort, intention, or care.

The future of creativity will depend on whether we accept this comfort or resist it. We can allow our imagination to be coddled — wrapped in convenience until it forgets how to feel — or we can choose the harder path of making, of friction, of becoming.

To create is to touch the world and be touched in return. It is to move through difficulty and emerge changed. That struggle is not a flaw in creativity; it is its foundation.

If coddled creativity promises a world without pain, it also threatens a world without growth. And a creativity that never struggles may never truly live.